Quiltmaking
Essentials 2

Settings and Borders, Backings and Bindings

Donna Lynn Thomas

Martingale®
Create with Confidence

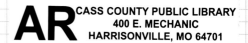

Dedication

To my beloved husband, Terry, who no matter what all is going on in our lives, manages to support me and still take care of the honey-do list. He always goes above and beyond. I don't know what I did to deserve him, but I sure am glad he's here beside me.

Quiltmaking Essentials 2:
Settings and Borders, Backings and Bindings
© 2015 by Donna Lynn Thomas

Martingale®
19021 120th Ave. NE, Ste. 102
Bothell, WA 98011-9511 USA
ShopMartingale.com

Printed in China

20 19 18 17 16 15   8 7 6 5 4 3 2 1

Library of Congress Cataloging-in-Publication Data is available upon request.

ISBN: 978-1-60468-542-8

On the Cover: "Gems" quilt from *Patchwork Palette* (Martingale, 2013).

Mission Statement

Dedicated to providing quality products and service to inspire creativity.

Credits

PUBLISHER AND CHIEF VISIONARY OFFICER
Jennifer Erbe Keltner

EDITORIAL DIRECTOR
Karen Costello Soltys

DESIGN DIRECTOR
Paula Schlosser

ACQUISITIONS EDITOR
Karen M. Burns

PRODUCTION MANAGER
Regina Girard

TECHNICAL EDITOR
Laurie Baker

COVER AND INTERIOR DESIGNER
Connor Chin

COPY EDITOR
Melissa Bryan

PHOTOGRAPHER
Brent Kane

ILLUSTRATOR
Anne Moscicki

Acknowledgments

A great deal of thanks and appreciation goes to my dear friends Kelly Ashton and Barb Eikmeier for generously donating photos of their own quilts as examples of various topics in this book. I've made just about every kind of quilt and quilt part possible, but there are a few exceptions and they filled the gaps for me. Thanks so much!

And I wouldn't be writing a pair of books like *Quiltmaking Essentials* if I hadn't had exceptional teachers along the way. Deep appreciation goes to my mother, my first teacher; Carla Hassel (*Super Quilter* books); Jessie MacDonald and Marian Shafer (*Let's Make a Patchwork Quilt*); and Jeannette Muir, for a very instructive workshop retreat early on when I was struggling for precision. The NQA certified teacher's program really forced me to fine-tune my teaching and precision skills as I prepared for certification back in the 1980s. Barbara Brackman's *Encyclopedia of Pieced Patterns* continues to be a source of inspiration, with its pages full of luscious old block designs that never seem to age.

Thanks to all of you for teaching me.

Contents

Introduction

Welcome to the second volume of the two-part *Quiltmaking Essentials* reference books! Hopefully you have the first volume, *Quiltmaking Essentials 1: Cutting and Piecing Skills* (Martingale, 2014), which provides information about mastering basic rotary cutting, machine piecing, pressing, and block assembly.

This volume continues where the first book left off and covers quilt settings, quilt-top assembly, sashing, plain and pieced borders, backings, and binding. In short, it teaches you how to put your blocks together to make a machine-pieced quilt top, addressing everything except the actual quilting process for finishing your quilts, which is an extensive topic already covered in many excellent books. Once again, emphasis is placed on mastering the skills so they become second nature and you can enjoy the process of making your quilts without frustration.

As in the first volume, I've separated the major subjects into their own sections for easy reference. Within each section there's a wealth of information. *Quiltmaking Essentials 2: Settings and Borders, Backings and Bindings* is meant to be your resource for more detailed how-to information than most books and patterns can include. To keep it affordably priced, you won't find any project instructions between these covers. There are plenty of pattern books out there that don't cover quiltmaking fundamentals, so think of these two volumes as companions you can use with all your quilting projects.

Whether you're a beginner who's growing in skill mastery, or a more advanced quilter looking to refresh seldom-used skills or looking for new ways to accomplish a goal, I hope you find answers to your questions within these pages. I don't imagine you'll read the book from cover to cover, but if you do, I think you'll find that the wealth of information I promised will be like discovering a pot of gold at the end of the rainbow—you'll be rich with knowledge.

My goal is for these two books to become well-worn with use over the years. Go ahead and dog-ear pages. Highlight information you use often. Write notes in the margins. Most of all, my wish is for you to master essential quiltmaking skills so you can enjoy many fun, frustration-free years of creating and sewing quilts you can be proud of!

Once you've sewn your blocks, you'll be anxious to get started on that quilt you want to make. But before you start laying out blocks willy-nilly, you need to know about the various ways you can "set" your blocks together.

First, if you haven't done so already, check the size of all your blocks to make sure the measurements are consistent. If you've been careful, they should be just about perfect in size with maybe a difference of ⅛" on occasion. (We *are* human!) If they're off by a small amount, you can probably ease them to fit.

If the block sizes differ widely and can't be trimmed to a common size without lopping off points, you may want to sew 2"-wide or larger framing strips around each block and then trim the framed blocks to a standard size. This may result in small visual discrepancies from framed block to framed block, but they won't be noticeable in the end. The framing strips can be muted or bold or anything in between. Be aware, though, that framing strips may not work with all quilt designs or setting arrangements. The best solution is to cut and sew accurately in the first place when making your blocks.

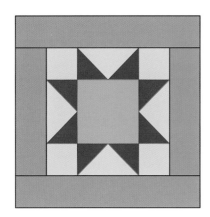

Block with oversized framing strips that will be trimmed to a standard size later.

Straight Settings

A straight-set arrangement is probably the easiest and most common way to set blocks together. The blocks are laid out in stacked horizontal rows, which are then sewn together to make the quilt center.

"Fractured Glass" reflects a simple straight setting, with the blocks placed next to each other.

Another option is to insert plain or pieced sashing strips between the blocks and rows. See "Sashing" (page 22) for more information on sashing strips.

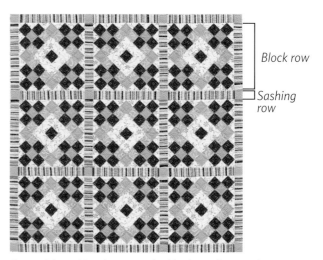

Block row

Sashing row

Even with sashing between the blocks and rows, the horizontal rows of blocks in "Spring Album" qualify it as a straight-set arrangement.

Determining the Number of Blocks in a Straight-Set Quilt Setting

Yes, this step involves some simple multiplication, but I assure you it's nothing that will have you running through the house with your hair on fire. You probably won't even need a calculator.

Single repeating block designs. When looking at the picture or diagram of a straight-set quilt composed of one repeating block, it's easy to calculate the total number of blocks in the quilt. Multiply the number of blocks across the top horizontally by the number of blocks along the side vertically. In the example shown, there are four blocks across the top and five down the side. The result of 4 x 5 tells us that this setting requires a total of 20 blocks.

"Pinwheel Shadow" features 20 blocks in a 4 by 5 setting.

Two-block alternating designs. The formula differs for two-block designs, depending on whether the total number of blocks is odd or even. Quilts with an odd number of blocks are more common and are recognized by placement of the same block in each of the four corners. For these quilts, you'll need an odd number of the block design that will be in the corners (which I'll call A), and one less—an even number—of the alternate block design (referred to here as B). For example, if your quilt setting is 5 x 5, requiring a total of 25 blocks, you will need 13 of block A and 12 of block B.

In order for the same block to appear at each corner of an alternating two-block design, you need an odd number of the block that goes in the corners and an even number of the alternating block, as in "Carrie's Box" shown here.

To calculate how many of each block design you need, multiply the number of blocks across the top horizontally by the number of blocks along the side vertically to determine the total number of blocks. Divide that number in half. Round up to the next whole number for block A; round down to the nearest whole number for block B. In our example, in which you need 25 blocks, 25 ÷ 2 = 12.5. Round up to 13 for block A, and round down to 12 for block B.

You can ignore this information for two-block quilt settings if your particular design doesn't require or you don't desire all four corners to be the same. In such a case, you'll have an equal number of each of the two blocks used in the quilt. They will still be arranged alternately in each row and from row to row, but the finished quilt will have an asymmetrical layout. Calculate the total number of blocks as described for single repeating block designs and divide the result by two to determine the number of each block.

Other block arrangements. Sometimes quilts include multiple block designs, such as a sampler quilt in which each block is different (see right). Another example is a quilt that features one block design made in multiple colors, with the colors arranged in diagonal bands across the quilt top (see below). There are many unique straight-set quilts that fall outside of the simple examples given above. In such cases, it's easiest to simply sit down and count what you need!

The sampler quilt below is an example of a straight setting in which each block is different.

Sampler quilt

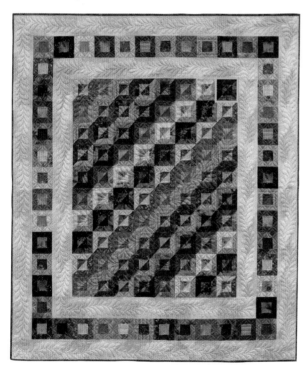

Although the layout is a simple straight setting, "Taupe Buttons" incorporates multiple colorations of the same block. Rather than trying to apply a mathematical formula to determine the number of blocks needed, it's easier to just count the number of each block color used.

Sewing Straight-Set Quilts

Although assembling a straight-set quilt is pretty straightforward, there are some guidelines to keep in mind.

Once your blocks are squared away (pun intended!), lay them out to form the rows in the quilt setting. Keeping them in order, sew them together to make each row. Press the seam allowances joining the blocks in one of the two ways shown on page 11. One approach may work better than the other depending on the number of seams or the design of your blocks. Only you can determine which is best for your particular blocks. The ultimate goal is for the seam allowances joining the blocks in each row to nest together when sewn to the next row.

Pressing option 1. Press all seam allowances in the same direction within each row, but alternate the direction from row to row.

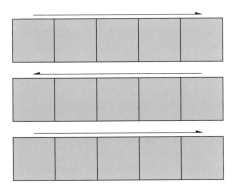

Block rows pressed in alternate directions from row to row.

Pressing option 2. Press seam allowances in alternating directions from block to block within each row as shown. This works especially well when you have heavily pieced blocks alternating with lightly pieced blocks or plain squares of fabric.

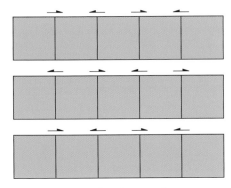

Blocks pressed in alternate directions within rows and between rows.

For sewing quilts that include sashing, see "Sashing" (page 22) for more information.

On-Point Settings

An on-point quilt setting, also referred to as a diagonal setting, is one in which the blocks are turned on their corners, or points, and sewn together in diagonal rows, rather than being assembled in horizontal or vertical rows. The blocks from a

straight-set quilt can look completely different when turned on point.

In "Warm Winds," traditional Windmill blocks are set on point without sashing, forming small pinwheels where the blocks meet.

As with straight-set layouts, on-point settings can include plain or pieced sashing inserted between the blocks and rows. See "Sashing" (page 22) for more information on both plain and pieced sashing.

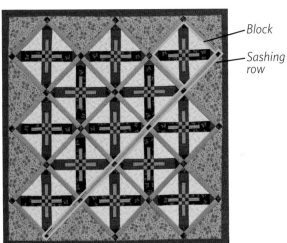

Block

Sashing row

The sashing strips and squares in an on-point quilt setting such as "High Rise" add a visual diagonal movement that counterbalances the vertical and horizontal flow of the blocks themselves.

Some innovative quilters, such as Sally Schneider, have devised a way to create the exterior rows of a diagonally set quilt from pieced blocks, thus mimicking a pieced border. Sally calls them built-in borders, because the borders are assembled right along with the rest of the quilt in diagonal rows.

Building the pieced borders into the blocks makes this quilt painless to assemble.

The built-in borders on this diagonally set "Stripple Star" quilt are in the blocks, pieced side setting triangles, and pieced corner setting triangles on the ends of the block rows. Look carefully and see if you can find them. Check out the illustration above right for the answer.

Determining the Number of Blocks in an On-Point Quilt Setting

On-point quilt settings have outside and inside sets, even if all the blocks are the same. The outside set (labeled A in the diagram) is composed of the blocks that fall on the corners of the quilt and alternate throughout the quilt top. (Note that the term "outside" also includes interior blocks.) The inside set (labeled B) consists of the interior blocks that alternate with the outside set.

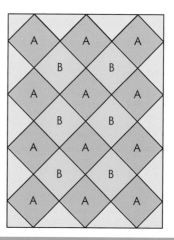

Single repeating block designs. In a quilt composed entirely of one repeating block, it's a simple matter to calculate how many total blocks you'll need for an on-point setting. First, multiply the number of blocks across the top horizontally by the number of blocks along the side vertically to determine the total number needed for the *outside* set. In the example shown on page 12, there are three across the top and four down the side for a 3 x 4 outside set. Multiply 3 x 4 for a total of 12 blocks.

To calculate the number of blocks needed for the inside set, subtract 1 from the number of blocks across the top and the number of blocks along the side, and multiply those numbers. So the 3 x 4 outside set in our previous example would indicate a 2 x 3 inside set. Multiply 2 x 3 for a total of six blocks.

Now add the outside-set and inside-set numbers for the total number of blocks needed for the quilt top. In our example, 12 + 6 indicates that 18 blocks are required in the on-point setting.

Two-block alternating designs. If you're using two different block designs in the quilt, generally one will make up the outside set (A) and the second will make up the inside set (B). Calculate the number needed in the same manner described for a single repeating block design.

Other block arrangements. If the quilt incorporates many block designs or block color variations, then it's easiest to just look at the quilt drawing and count out how many you'll need of each.

Setting Triangles

When the diagonal rows of on-point quilt settings are sewn together, they result in uneven edges. To make the quilt top a nice, even square or rectangle, it's necessary to add large side setting triangles to the ends of the rows. Smaller setting triangles are added to the corners of the quilt center after the rows are joined.

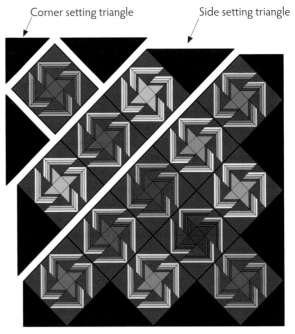

Corner setting triangle   Side setting triangle

The large black triangles on the ends of the on-point block rows in this "Star Trails" quilt are called side setting triangles. The smaller ones that square off the quilt center are corner setting triangles.

Side setting triangles. Quarter-square triangles are used on the ends of the rows in on-point settings. These triangles are created by cutting a square into quarters diagonally, resulting in triangles with the straight of grain on the long edge. To prevent your quilt top from stretching out of shape, it's important to place this long, straight-of-grain edge along the outer edge of the quilt center.

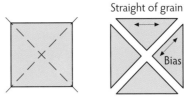

Straight of grain

Bias

Quarter-square triangles

For quilts in which the side setting triangle will be joined to a block (rather than a sashing piece), the finished length of the triangle's long edge needs to be the same as the diagonal measurement of the finished block. Therefore, you must calculate that diagonal measurement first, and then figure out how big you need to cut the parent square in order to produce side setting triangles of the correct size. (Refer to "Sashing for On-Point Quilts" to calculate the size of the parent square for quilts with sashing.)

The diagonal of a block is equal to the finished block size x 1.414. So multiply the *finished* size of your block (don't include the outer seam allowances) by 1.414 and round this number to the nearest ⅛". Then add 1¼" for seam allowances. For example, if your finished block measures 9", multiply 9" x 1.414 to get 12.726". Round that up to the nearest ⅛" to get 12.75" (12¾"), and then add 1.25" (1¼") for seam allowances to calculate the size of the parent square (12.75" + 1.25" = 14").

Some quilters prefer to cut oversized side setting triangles and then trim the excess after joining the quilt-top rows. To do that, multiply the finished block size by 1.5 and add 1½" instead of 1¼" for seam allowances.

Each parent square will yield four side setting triangles. To calculate how many squares to cut, count the total number of side setting triangles you need, divide by four, and then round up to the nearest whole number.

Corner setting triangles. Corner setting triangles are created by cutting a parent square in half diagonally to make two half-square triangles. Position the triangles so that the straight of grain falls on the edge of the quilt top.

Straight
of grain

Bias

So, how do you figure the size of the parent square, you ask? The short edge of the corner triangle is half the length of the diagonal measurement of the block, so that's where you need to start. Multiply the finished block size by 0.71 (which magically is half of 1.414 after rounding up!), and round up this number to the nearest ⅛". Then add ⅞" for seam allowances. Let's use a 12" block as an example. Multiply 12" x 0.71 to get 8.52". Round that up to the nearest ⅛" to get 8.625" (8⅝"), and then add .875" (⅞") for seam allowances to calculate the size of the parent square to cut (8.625" + .875" = 9.5", or 9½"). Cut two squares this size and cut them in half diagonally to make four corner triangles—two from each square. If you prefer oversized triangles, multiply the finished block size by 0.75 and add 1" instead of ⅞" for seam allowances. That will give you some leeway for squaring up your quilt top later.

Sewing On-Point Quilts

Once you've cut your side and corner setting triangles, lay them out with your blocks in diagonal rows. Sew the pieces in each row together, aligning the bottom edge of each triangle with the bottom edge of the block to which it's attached. Just as with straight-set quilts (see "Sewing Straight-Set Quilts" on page 10), you can choose to press the seam allowances in alternating directions from row to row, or in alternating directions from block to block within each row.

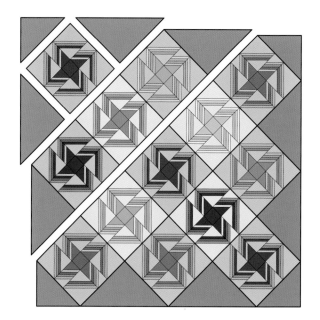

Once the rows are sewn together, add the corner triangles to the quilt top. Trim the outside edges of the quilt top to ¼" from the block corners so you'll have straight edges on which to align any borders or binding strips.

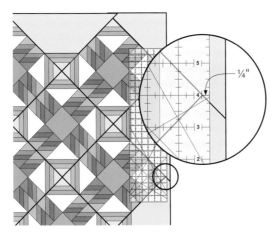

Some quilters intentionally make their setting triangles considerably oversized to create the illusion that the blocks are "floating," as shown in illustration below. To do so, measure and trim a consistent distance from the block corners so the triangle edges are neat and even in size.

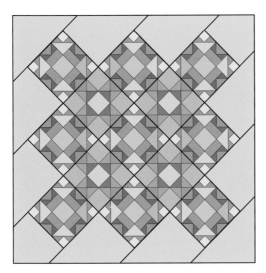

Oversized setting triangles make the blocks appear to float in the quilt center.

Another option is to make pieced setting triangles, adding an extra visual element to your diagonally set quilt.

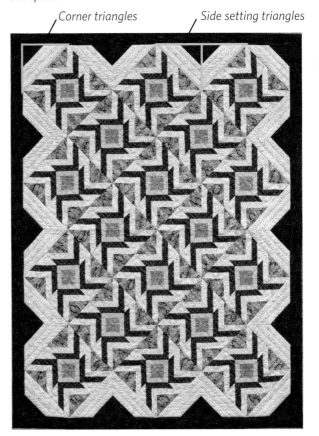

The side setting triangles in "Blades" are composed of two large white half-square triangles with black squares sewn onto the corners diagonally, and then trimmed to create a black point. Pairs of the white-and-black triangles are sewn together to form the larger side setting triangles.

Vertical Row Settings

Vertical block arrangements are a fun alternative to straight and on-point quilt settings. Sew blocks together straight or on-point (combined with setting triangles) in vertical rows and then join the rows, alternating them with vertical spacer strips of fabric if you wish. Of course, you can add sashing between the blocks, or piece the spacer strips between the rows. There are all kinds of fun things you can do with a vertical row setting.

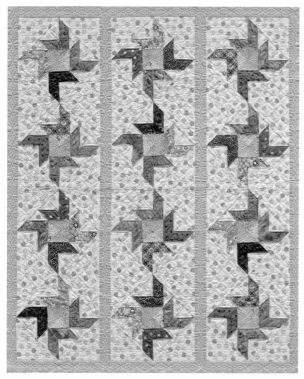

This simple vertical strip quilt, "Cupid's Arrows," is composed of blocks set on point in vertical columns, alternating with green bands. It's very simple but a nice alternative to a straight-set quilt.

The only difference between a vertical setting and a straight or on-point setting is that the blocks are assembled in vertical columns instead of horizontal or diagonal rows. As always, check to make sure your blocks are accurately sized. Blocks may be sewn together straight or on point. If they're set on

point, you'll need to make side and corner setting triangles for each row just as with an on-point quilt. (Refer to "Setting Triangles" on page 13.) Remember to trim the strip edges to ¼" from the block points just as with an on-point quilt setting.

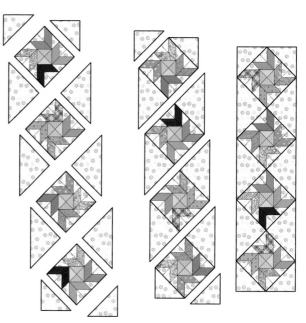

Sew the blocks together into columns and then sew the columns together, alternating them with any plain or pieced vertical strips as called for in the design.

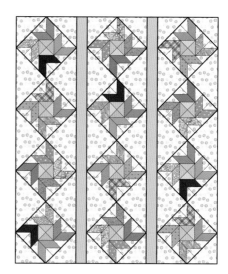

Sometimes the block strips are offset with spacer strips at the top and bottom of the columns, and then the columns are sewn directly together. The sky's the limit to your creativity when using a vertical strip quilt setting.

Horizontal Row-by-Row Settings

This type of setting is essentially a vertical set turned on its side. Instead of being assembled in vertical columns, the blocks are assembled into horizontal rows with or without plain or pieced strips between them. The same blocks may be used in each row, but more often than not, each row is a bit different. For instance, one row may consist of house blocks and the next row tree blocks. This setting is frequently used for group round-robins, with each participant adding a new row to the quilt she or he receives, and then passing it on to the next person for the addition of another unique row. You never know what you'll end up with, but you can be sure it will be creative and one of a kind. Again, sewing these rows together is no different than sewing a straight-set quilt.

This vibrant, sophisticated quilt, "Painted Mountains" made by Kelly Ashton, repeats the same block but in different colors, arranging them in a chevron design in a horizontal strip setting.

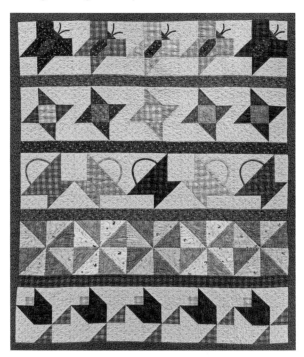

Horizontal row-by-row settings often have a variety of blocks in each row, as shown in this sweet sampler made by children. "Cousins by the Row" was made by cousins Anna Martin, Becky Martin, Sarah Eikmeier, David Martin, and Eric Eikmeier.

Unequal-Sized Block Settings

Another popular setting is one in which blocks of varying sizes are sewn together to make the quilt top. Although blocks can be made specifically for this type of quilt, this setting is also a good way to combine blocks from different sources: leftover orphan blocks from other projects, blocks acquired in a guild exchange, blocks received as gifts from friends, or even those purchased at an estate sale.

The ultimate goal is to sew the blocks into groups that will form rows or larger pieced sections, and then join these components to complete the quilt top. The key to putting odd sizes together is to find a common dimension they can all be geared to. For instance, blocks that are all divisible by 3 work well together: 3", 6", 9", 12". You can do the same with blocks divisible by 2, 4, or 5.

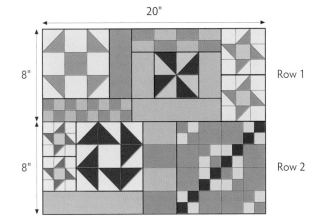

For unequal block sizes, fill in with smaller units to make rows of consistent size.

If needed, add framing strips to bring some blocks or block groups up to an adequate size, or pair two smaller blocks together and set them next to a larger block. Sometimes pieced or plain strips are added between or around blocks to create the common size. You're limited only by your creativity.

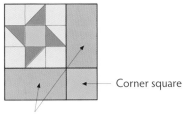

Corner square

Fill with patches, smaller blocks or fabric strips.

Medallion Settings

Medallion settings begin with a single block or a few pieced blocks in the center of the quilt. The center can be set straight or on point, but either way, the quilt is built by adding successive rounds of borders and/or pieced corner triangles until the quilt is the size you want. Usually the components of each border are different, and appliqué is often added to the process in various places. Medallion quilts can be simple or quite complex and striking. The key to a successful medallion quilt is accurate cutting and sewing in order for all the components to match perfectly.

Four pieced blocks form the center of "Rose Medallion." Multiple pieced and plain borders were built around the center.

Medallions Make the Rounds

A medallion setting is quite popular for round-robin quilts. The person who will eventually own the quilt contributes the center, and then the project passes sequentially to each member of the group, who adds a new and different border or setting element to what he or she receives. Some groups impose rules or guidelines for each border, while others do not.

I made this "Antique Rose" quilt as a medallion round-robin with my Army-wife quilting friends stationed at Fort Leavenworth in the mid-1990s. We each made our own center, and other participants added the subsequent borders. It was a fun challenge with a delightful outcome.

Overall Designs

Not all great quilt arrangements rely on blocks. Some quilts are composed of pieces that are all sewn together, or the pieces are joined into sections that are then joined to make the whole design. Good examples of this type of construction are Double Wedding Ring, Seven Sisters, hexagon quilts, and quilts made using other 60° units.

Sometimes overall designs require set-in seams. These seams are necessary when the only way to add a piece to a block is by stitching it in place in two steps, such as when joining hexagons. As you can see in the example below, the loose hexagon is set into the larger unit by first sewing one side of the hexagon and then the other.

This stunning quilt, "Constellation" designed by Kelly Ashton, is a beautiful example of allover construction. Figuring out how it was put together is pretty tricky; the secret is Y-seams and pieced hexagons that build into larger sections.

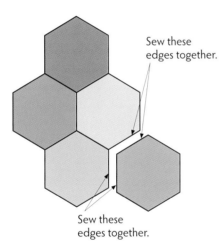

Sew these edges together.

Sew these edges together.

Set in hexagons with Y-seams, building the design as you go.

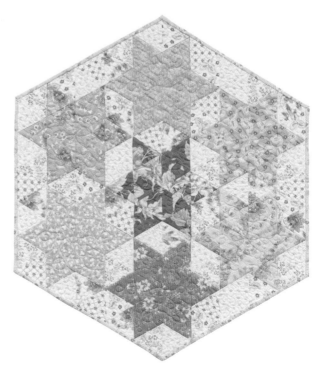

This "Seven Sisters" quilt consists of a series of equilateral triangles laid out and joined directly into rows, which are then sewn together. The use of color defines the stars, but no stars are actually sewn together, as you can see in the illustration on page 21.

Stars in the "Seven Sisters" quilt are formed by sewing together equilateral triangles—and careful color placement.

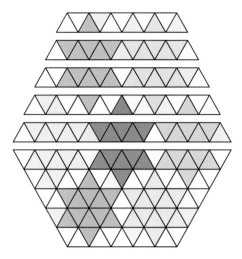

The Double Wedding Ring pattern is another example of an allover design. To achieve this design, pieced arcs and four-pointed star shapes are sewn together successively to create the quilt. As the sections come together they mimic a row-type construction, but they aren't quite the same because the seams aren't straight across from side to side.

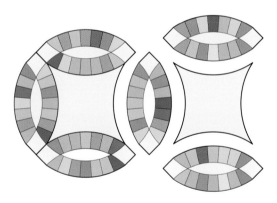

You may encounter many other types of overall designs as you look through magazines, patterns, and books. Once you recognize the overall design, replicating it in your own project is a simple matter of identifying the basic unit and method of construction.

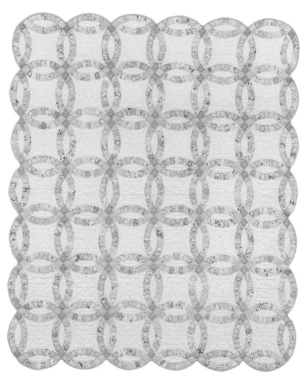

Always a favorite, Double Wedding Ring quilts are pieced in arcs, which are then sewn around the white centers. No row-by-row construction is involved. Sections are sewn and then built onto the quilt. Some quilters build out from one corner while others stick to a quasi row-by-row process. This example is "Mamo's Double Wedding Ring" by Edna Bertha Steven Ashton, circa 1935; from the collection of Kelly Ashton.

Types of Sashing

Sashing strips are pieces sewn between blocks within a row, and they may be used between rows as well.

Sashing can consist of plain fabric strips or pieced strips, and you'll find it in both straight and on-point quilt settings. It can run across an entire quilt top as one piece, or be sewn into rows with sashing squares located at the corners of each block.

Although sashing strips run between blocks and rows, some quilt designers choose to make the first border on their straight-set quilt a sashing border. A sashing border is one that mimics the sashing between the blocks. It can be either pieced or plain, but it will match the block sashing. You don't usually find sashing borders used in on-point quilt settings, because the side setting triangles separate the center of the quilt from the first border.

Below and on the following page are some examples of different types of sashing.

This lovely "Split Geese" quilt has sashing with sashing squares but no sashing border.

You'll see pieced sashing not only between the blocks of this "Cool Blue" quilt, but also in the sashing border.

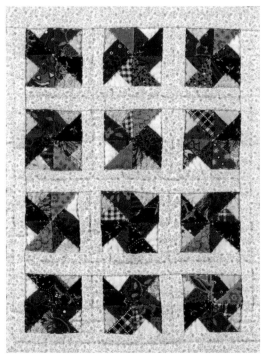

Although this is a miniature quilt, "Scrap Windmill" has all the components of a larger quilt, including plain sashing without sashing squares but with a sashing border.

On-point quilts, such as "Autumn Leaves," are just as likely to have plain sashing without sashing squares as straight-set quilts.

The sashing strips and squares in this lovely diagonally set "Delft Baskets" quilt are made from a variety of different prints.

Sashing strips and sashing squares are sometimes pieced in such a way that they integrate with the block corners to make secondary designs. This creates the look of interlocking blocks, making it difficult to discern where the blocks begin and end.

Look closely at this "Morris Star" quilt. It contains only nine blocks, but the sashing and sashing squares are pieced to mimic the blocks, creating the look of interlocking blocks.

Here are a few examples of commonly used pieced sashing strips with complementary sashing squares.

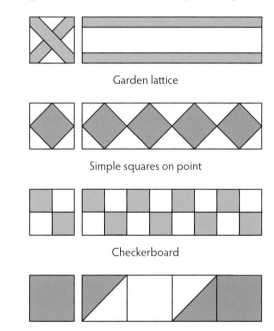

Garden lattice

Simple squares on point

Checkerboard

Star forms at the corner where four sashing units meet

Sometimes pieced sashing can be used to create a larger overall design element, as in the traditional Storm at Sea design.

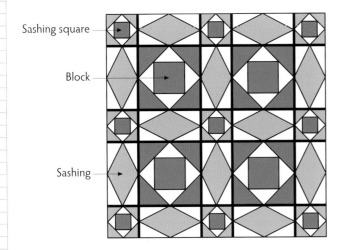

Sashing square

Block

Sashing

Sewing Quilts with Sashing

General cutting and sewing rules apply when including sashing in your quilt setting, whether the sashing is plain or pieced.

- **Wait to cut your sashing strips until after your blocks are finished.** Sometimes the fabric you had planned for your sashing may not meet your expectations after you've previewed it with your blocks on a design wall, "design bed," or "design floor." Or, you may decide you don't want sashing at all, or you might want to add a pieced sashing, or remove sashing corner squares. Because sashing can be a bold or subtle design element, it's best to wait and see if it will be what you want or if you want to make changes.

- **Check the accuracy of both the blocks** and plain or pieced sashing strips. Trim everything to size, removing any stray dog-ears and cleaning up edges.

- **Adjust the size of the plain sashing strips to fit the actual size** of your blocks, if your finished blocks aren't the size they should be. This isn't an ideal situation, but it happens. If you're working with picced sashing you can ease in small block discrepancies by pinning in any fullness and sewing with the longer part on the bottom next to the feed dogs. Sometimes you can also take in or let out small amounts on multiple sashing seams to make them fit the block size. Large discrepancies may require a new sashing plan. You always want to sew as precisely as possible so you aren't fudging to make things fit.

- **Always press seam allowances toward the sashing** when assembling quilt tops with sashing, especially those with sashing squares. This rule applies regardless of whether you're sewing blocks and sashing into rows or sewing rows and sashing strips together. Any seam with a sashing should be pressed toward the sashing. This ensures that the seam allowances will nest at all the intersections where they meet. You want to use those nesting seams to create sharp, perfect corners at the intersections. It also prevents any bulk from being pressed under the pieced blocks.

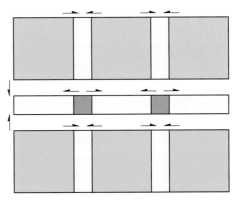

Press all seam allowances toward the sashing for easy seam matching.

- **Strive for perfectly aligned seams when sewing sashing strips to your quilt,** regardless of whether the quilt setting is straight or on point. Sashing with corner squares naturally keeps the seam lines square and visually continuous. Sashing strips without corner squares require extra care to ensure that sashing appears to be continuous where the strips visually cross each other.

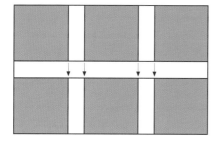

Sashing seams must form a visually continuous line.

Sewing Sashing without Corner Squares

When sewing sashing without corner squares, follow these steps to make sure the sashing seams fall directly across from each other.

1. On the wrong side of each short sashing strip sewn into the first block row, lay a ruler along one of the sashing seams so that it reaches across the long sashing strip to the opposite raw edge. Make a mark on the raw edge of the long sashing strip.

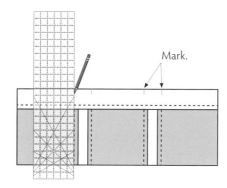

Mark.

2. When aligning the next block row to the long sashing strip, match and pin the short sashing

seams of the new row to the seam marks on the edge of the long sashing strip.

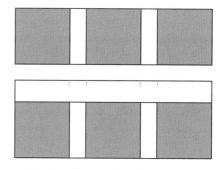

Match and pin marks on long sashing to sashing seam intersections on next row.

Sashing for Straight-Set Quilts

Lay out the blocks, sashing strips, and any corner squares as desired. Sew the blocks and sashing strips together in alternating positions to create block rows. Sew sashing strips and any sashing squares alternately into sashing rows. Press seam allowances toward the sashing strips.

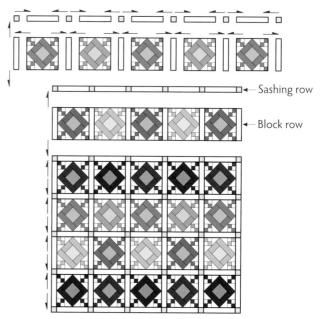

Sashing row

Block row

To complete the center of the quilt, sew the block rows and sashing rows together in alternating positions, pressing seam allowances toward the sashing rows.

Sashing for On-Point Quilts

Lay out the blocks, sashing strips, any sashing squares, and side and corner setting triangles into diagonal rows. When including sashing in an on-point setting, the sashing must be sewn together alternately with the blocks to form diagonal block rows. Sew sashing and any sashing squares together to form alternating sashing rows just as with straight-set quilts. Add the setting triangles to the ends of the rows before joining the rows to complete the quilt center. Be careful to orient the triangles correctly at the row ends.

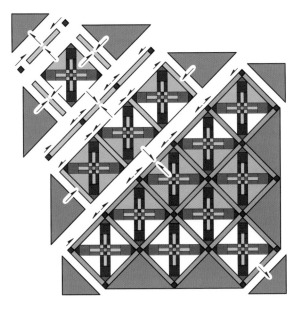

When calculating the size of the side setting triangles for an on-point quilt with sashing, you must include the sashing-strip width in your finished block size. Look at the example above right. The finished sizes of the block and sashing strip are 12" and 2", respectively. Therefore, when you're calculating the size of the parent square that you'll need for quarter-square side setting triangles, add one sashing width to your block size (12" + 2" = 14") to determine your finished block size. Then proceed as described for side setting triangles in "Setting Triangles" on page 13 to calculate the size square you need.

For corner triangles, add two times the sashing width to the block size (12" + 2" + 2" = 16"), and then proceed as described for corner setting triangles in "Setting Triangles" to calculate the size of the parent square you need for the corner triangles.

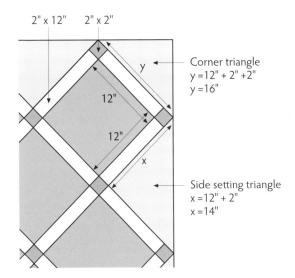

Sashing can be a lot of fun in a quilt, adding visual interest, surprising design elements, or just plain restful space between heavily pieced blocks. Consider using them in your own quilt designs.

Borders

Borders can be as simple as plain strips of fabric that surround the center of the quilt, or they can be much more elaborate and involve as much piecing as the quilt center itself. Think of borders as the equivalent of the various colors and widths of mats used to surround a framed painting or photograph. The ultimate goal is to enhance the center of the quilt. For some quilts, one border may be perfect, while other quilts will benefit from several borders, and still others may not need any border at all.

No matter how many or few borders you plan to add to your quilt, it's important to press your quilt top so it's smooth and wrinkle-free before you start. Square up the four corners to 90° and trim any excess to ¼" from points that fall on the edge, if you haven't already done so (refer to "Sewing On-Point Quilts" on page 14). At this point you should be able to tell if your top is lying flat. If it isn't, now's the time to figure out what's wrong and correct it. Adding border after border to a rippling, uneven quilt will only make the problem worse.

Once your quilt top is prepared you can start auditioning borders. Don't forget to consider the border corner treatment in your total look. Corners can be butted to create squared corners, include a square (plain or pieced), or be mitered. You'll see various types throughout this section.

When it comes to actually sewing the borders to the quilt top, generally the side borders are added first, followed by the top and bottom borders.

Plain Borders

Plain border strips can be cut from either the lengthwise grain of the fabric (parallel to the selvage) or from the crosswise grain of the fabric (selvage to selvage). There are things to consider when deciding which way to cut. For instance, if you're using a striped or directional print, which way is best for your design needs? The stripes or motifs will run differently if you cut one way instead of the other.

Directional prints will look different when cut on the crosswise or lengthwise grains.

Do you want a directional print positioned so the motifs or stripes all run in the same direction no matter which side of the quilt they're on? In that case, you need to cut both lengthwise and crosswise strips in order to orient the motif in the correct direction on all four borders.

Use a combination of crosswise and lengthwise strips when you want a directional print to face the same direction on all sides.

Another consideration is whether you have enough fabric yardage to cut the full length of the longest border strips parallel to the selvage. If you're working from your stash and only have two yards (72") of the intended border print, you can't cut a 94" lengthwise border strip. But you do have options. If you have enough fabric width, you could cut lengthwise strips and piece them together to make a long enough strip. Just make sure you have enough width across the fabric to cut all of your strips. Your other option is to cut crosswise strips and sew them together to make longer strips. Again, you'll need to make sure you have enough yardage to cut the required number of strips.

Crosswise Border Strips

Crosswise border strips are cut from selvage to selvage and, if necessary, sewn together end to end to make the necessary strip length to fit the sides of the quilt.

Calculating What You Need

Before you do any cutting, calculate how many strips you need and how much yardage this will require. The strip width is the desired border width plus ½" for seam allowances.

Let's use the example of adding 6"-wide *finished* borders to a quilt top with a *finished* measurement of 50" x 60" before the borders are added.

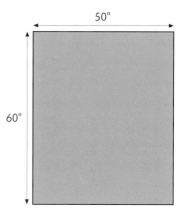

Quilt top *finishes* to
50" wide and 60" long.

1. Add the quilt width and length together and double it. In this case, 50" + 60" = 110" x 2 = 220". That's the circumference of your quilt top up to this point.

2. Multiply the finished border width by four, and add that to the circumference: 6" border width x 4 = 24" + 220" = 244". Add about 10" to this number for the loss incurred when joining seams and as well as for potential motif positioning requirements, and you reach a grand total of 254" of border-strip length needed.

3. Divide the result from step 2 by 40", which is the usable width of fabric you should count on. The result is the number of border strips you need to cut. In this case the result is seven strips (254 ÷ 40 = 6.35 strips, rounded up to 7). You may find you need fewer strips if your fabric has a usable width greater than 40", but it's best to err on the side of caution as opposed to coming up short.

4. To calculate the yardage you need for these strips, multiply the number of strips by the *cut* size (finished size plus ½" for seam allowances) of the border strips: 7 strips x 6½" = 45½", which is a bit over 1¼ yards. Round up your result to the nearest ⅛ yard (1⅜ yards) to give yourself some room for straightening and errors.

Cutting Crosswise Border Strips

Now you're ready to cut your crosswise border strips. Here are some tips for success.

- When cutting these strips, it's *very important* to make sure each and every cut is at a right angle to the folds of the fabric. If not, you'll end up with bent or V-shaped strips at the folds when they're opened out. Use two rulers to create the first clean-cut edge. Then cut the border strips, making sure there's always a horizontal ruler line on the fold with each cut. When you can no longer align both horizontal and vertical lines, it's time to make a new clean-cut edge.

- If the strip is wider than your ruler, use two rulers to build more width, using the longest one for the final cut. Again, have horizontal lines on the folds to ensure a right-angle cut.

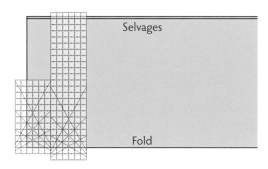

- Remove the selvages from the ends of the strips before using them.

Joining Crosswise Border Strips

When you need more border-strip length than one strip will yield, sew all the crosswise strips together end to end to make one long piece, and then crosscut the assorted strip lengths you need for all four sides of the quilt top. Sewing all the strips together end to end, rather than sewing just enough strips to achieve the required length for one side, maximizes the efficient use of the fabric strips. It also ensures that the border seams fall randomly on the sides of the quilt, making them less noticeable.

There are two ways to sew the strip seams together—with a straight seam or a diagonal seam. There are reasons for both, with pros and cons. The best way to see which type of seam will work best is

to preview it. Lay two strips together with one folded in half on top of the other mimicking a straight seam. Then lay out two more strips with one folded at a 90° angle to mimic a diagonal seam. Which one is most effective at hiding the seam? Sew your seam with whichever works best for your fabric.

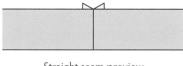

Straight seam preview

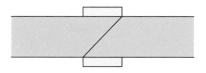

Diagonal seam preview

Straight seams. The simplest way to sew border strips together end to end is with a regular ¼" seam allowance. This is the best method when you have a limited amount of fabric. It's also the best way to sew together directional stripes or prints so that they will run perpendicular to the sides of the quilt. You can pin and match the repeat in the stripe or motif so there is no interruption in the pattern and the seam will be virtually hidden.

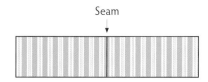

1. Sew the cut strips just as you would normally with a precise ¼" seam allowance.

2. Continue sewing all the strips end to end until you have one long pieced border strip.

3. Press the seam allowances to one side or the other, not open. A seam that's been pressed open is a weaker seam and also allows batting to pull through over time.

Diagonal seams. Diagonal seams use more strip length than straight seams, and I think they're a bit more prone to stretching because the stitching is on the bias. On the other hand, a diagonal seam is sometimes less conspicuous than a straight seam. If you choose a diagonal seam, quilting can be used to add stability and help counteract the tendency to stretch.

1. Lay one strip right side up and positioned horizontally. Layer the second strip right side down vertically so the ends of the two strips cross each other. Don't match the corners, but rather have the ends sticking out past the sides of the strips as shown. Pin the strips together diagonally.

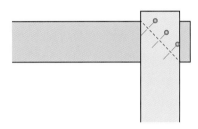

2. Sew precisely from the upper corner to the lower outside corner as shown. Stop with your needle down in the end of the seam. Without removing the strips from the machine, set up the tail end of the second strip with the third strip in the same fashion as the first. Chain sew the remaining diagonal seams.

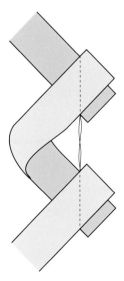

Chain sew diagonal seams joining border strips.

3. When all seams are sewn, remove the kite tail from your machine, cut the thread twists that connect them, and trim away the excess triangle ¼" from each seam.

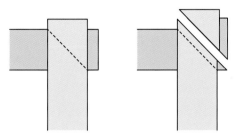

4. Press seam allowances to one side and you're ready to start cutting border lengths for your quilt top. Refer to "Borders with Butted Corners and Corner Squares" on page 34 and "Borders with Mitered Corners" on page 36 for information on how to measure, cut, and sew borders to quilt tops.

Lengthwise Border Strips

Lengthwise border strips are cut to the full length needed (no seaming required!) by cutting strips parallel to the fabric's selvage edge. This means you'll need enough yardage to cut the longest border strip required. Make sure you have more than enough fabric to cut a slightly longer strip than you need, especially if you'll be mitering the corners (refer to "Borders with Mitered Corners" on page 36).

Because most (but not all) printed fabric designs run from selvage to selvage, you must be careful that a lengthwise cut on a strongly directional print will be what you want. Preview it first! If the directional print runs parallel to the selvage, you'll need to buy at least a half yard more to accommodate the need to shift and cut the strip so the repeat or motif in the print falls where you want it. You don't necessarily have to position the motifs identically on each border strip, but you may not want a row of whole motifs on one border strip while another strip contains motifs that have been sliced through the center.

You may also want to consider sewing borders cut from a directional print, using either corner squares (see page 35) or a mitered corner seam (see page 36). Or, you can sew the borders in place without either of those options, arranging the border motif to fall attractively at the corners.

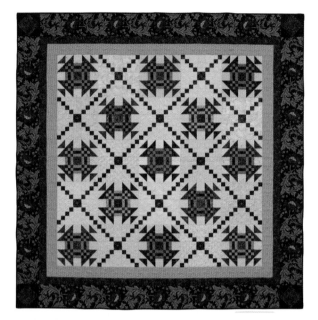

The lovely directional print in the outer border of this "Goose Chase" quilt didn't lend itself well to a mitered turn, so I pieced corner squares as an alternative.

The sunflower border print shown here in "Back in Time" had a bit of a primitive look, so it was fun to run it in bands around the quilt to create butted corners.

Cutting lengthwise border strips is a bit different from cutting crosswise strips. Rather than folding your fabric selvage to selvage as you would for crosswise strips, fold it raw edge to raw edge. Fold it again and again, carefully matching selvage edges, until you have no more than 23" of width from fold to fold. For long borders, you may end up with five or more layers, so make sure your rotary-cutting blade is new and sharp. Press with an iron so the fabric lies flat without wrinkles and the folds are even and smooth.

Fabric folded in layers with selvages aligned.

1. Remove the selvage from one side, creating a clean-cut edge.

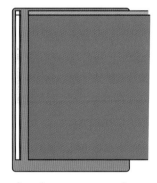

Remove the selvage to create a clean-cut edge.

2. Measure from the clean-cut edge and cut four border strips the desired width. Be sure to keep a horizontal ruler line on the folds while cutting to ensure a good right-angle cut.

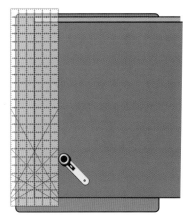

Cut border strips from the lengthwise grain.

3. Trim one end of the strip perpendicular to the cut edges to make a clean-cut edge. From this edge, measure in the required length for the border, including ½" for seam allowances. Trim the excess strip from the other end. For extra-long borders, use a measuring tape, securing it at one end and marking the desired length with a pin on the other end. Trim each strip to the desired length.

Measure the border length, including ½" for seams.
Mark with a pin; trim to the correct length.

Borders with Butted Corners and Corner Squares

There are three ways to handle the corners when adding borders to your quilt top: butted or squared corners, corner squares, or mitered corners. We'll discuss squared corners and corner squares in this section.

Mitered corners have more considerations, so I've given this treatment its own section, beginning on page 36.

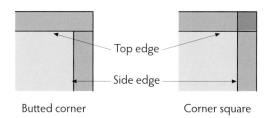

Butted corner   Corner square

Borders with Butted Corners

This is a very easy way to sew on borders and an application you'll see frequently. This style of border assembly is also referred to as "butted borders" or "lapped borders." Either cut your border strips from the lengthwise grain, or piece them to the desired length from crosswise-grain strips. Follow these easy instructions to sew the borders in place.

1. Measure the length of your quilt top through the center.

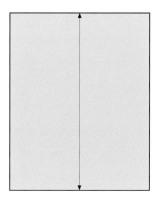

Center length

2. Cut two border strips to this length for the quilt sides. If you're working with end-to-end pieced border strips, make sure that a seam joining the strips won't fall within 6" of the corner. Adjust your cut from the border strips to accommodate a seam if necessary.

3. Sew these border strips to the sides of the quilt top. Press the seam allowances toward the border strips.

4. Finally, measure the center width of your quilt top, including the newly attached side borders. Follow the same procedures as above to cut two border strips, and pin one strip to the top edge and one strip to the bottom edge of the quilt top. Sew the borders in place. Press the seam allowances toward the border strips.

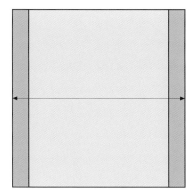

Center width

Ease to Appease

If the edges of the quilt top are slightly longer than the border strips, ease the borders to fit. Pin the ends of the border strip and quilt top together first, and then match the center of the quilt side to the center of the border. Keep halving and pinning subsequently smaller parts of the seam until all the fullness is eased in and equally distributed across the length of the quilt. If there's too much fullness to ease, figure out what went wrong, fix it, and try pinning the border again. A small amount of fullness is not uncommon, but there shouldn't be a lot. This technique can be used on all of the quilt edges. Ease to fit for small discrepancies, but fix the problem if there are large differences.

Borders with Corner Squares

Borders with corner squares are relatively easy to construct. Corner squares can add visually to a quilt by bringing another color from the quilt center out to the border. Corner squares are also useful in pieced borders, allowing a border design to continue around a corner. They can provide an alternative to

mitering a centered border design by providing an interruption or break to the design at the corner as discussed above.

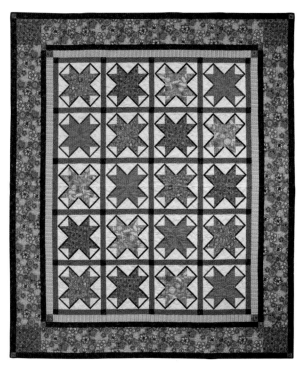

The border corner squares stop the striped inner border at the corners, while serving to bring the orange of the quilt center back out to the edges in "Star Light, Star Bright."

In "Warm by the Fire," the red-and-black stars surrounding the blocks are part of a pieced border. The pieced corner squares continue the design around the corners.

The process for measuring and cutting border strips is very much the same as for plain borders with squared corners.

1. Measure the center length of your quilt top and cut two border strips to this length, being careful that no joining seams will fall within 6" of the corner as described for borders with butted corners (page 34). Measure the center width of your quilt top and cut two border strips to this length.

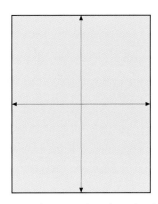

Measure the center length *and* width.

2. Cut or piece four corner squares so that their width and length is the same as the width of your border strip. For example, if your border strip is cut 6½" wide, your four corner squares should be 6½" x 6½".

3. Sew the first two border strips to the sides of the quilt top as described for borders with squared corners. Press the seam allowances toward the border strips.

4. Sew a corner square to each end of the remaining two border strips. Press the seam allowances toward the border strips.

5. Sew the borders with corner squares to the top and bottom edges of the quilt top, matching the corner-square seams with the side-border seams. By always pressing toward the border strips, you ensure that these seams will nest where they meet.

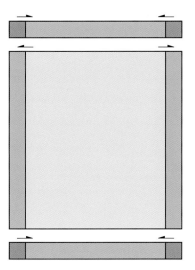

Borders with Mitered Corners

Borders with mitered corners have seams that are sewn from the inner corner diagonally to the outer corner. They can help visually move directional prints around a corner or otherwise provide a fine finish to many quilts by eliminating any vertical or horizontal seams, especially if the border strips are cut from the lengthwise grain. Cut them from either crosswise or lengthwise strips, depending on your needs and preferences.

Mitered corner

The directional print used in this, "Stars Dipped in Chocolate" border also appears in the sashing. Mitering the corners keeps the print moving around the quilt without interruption.

The vast majority of mitered quilt corners are sewn onto quilts with square (90°) corners. Some cases of hexagonal or octagonal quilts require mitered corners as well, as I'll discuss a bit later.

Simple Mitered Corners

These corners do not involve matching directional prints, so they're the easiest to execute. They're perfect for large, random overall prints without any direction to them. For information on mitering corners with directional prints, refer to "Mitering Corners with Border Prints" on page 39.

Cutting Border Strips for Simple Mitered Corners

Follow these basic steps to cut simple mitered borders without a directional print for your square-cornered quilt top. Let's use the example of a quilt top with a finished measurement of 40" x 60" to which we're going to sew a 4"-wide finished border with a mitered corner seam.

1. On the wrong side of the quilt top, use a pencil to mark a line ¼" from both adjacent sides of each corner to make two lines that intersect. Also mark the center of each side of the quilt top.

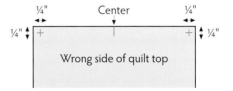

Mark ¼" from both edges of all four corners.

2. Measure the finished center length and finished center width of your quilt top, not including seam allowances. Write down these numbers.

3. Double the intended border width and write it down. For our example using a 4"-wide border, you would write down 8 (4 x 2 = 8).

4. Add the doubled border-width dimension to the center-length dimension for the side borders and to the center-width dimension for the top and bottom borders. Add ½" to each result for seam allowances. These are the lengths to cut your border strips. Write down these two numbers. Here are the calculations for our example:

   Side borders: 60" + 8" + ½" = 68½"
   Top and bottom borders: 40" + 8" + ½" = 48½"

5. Cut two strips the length required for the side borders and two strips the length required for the top and bottom borders. If you need to piece strips to make the appropriate length, sew the strips end to end first with either a straight seam or a diagonal seam, and then measure and cut.

6. On the wrong side of each strip, measure in from the end a distance equal to the border width plus ¼" and make a pencil mark on the border-strip edge that will be sewn to the quilt top. Also mark the center of each border strip.

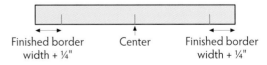

Finished border width + ¼"   Center   Finished border width + ¼"

Sewing Border Strips to Quilt Top for Mitered Corners

Sewing the strips in place for borders with mitered corners is not quite the same as working with border strips in the previous corner treatments we've discussed.

1. Working with one border at a time and with right sides together, match the pencil marks near the end of one border strip to the ¼" marks on the quilt-top corners on the appropriate edge of the quilt. Repeat for the opposite end. When done, two tails should extend past the quilt corners on both ends that measure the border width plus ¼". Match and pin the center marks of the border and quilt top. Pin the rest of the border to the top, distributing any fullness across the full width of the side.

2. Begin sewing at the matched ¼" marks and stop at the matched ¼" marks on the other end of the border. *Do not sew from raw edge to raw edge.* Backstitch at the beginning and end of the seam.

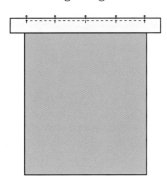

3. Repeat the process to match, pin, and sew the remaining three borders in place. At the four corners, the stitching lines from each seam should meet perfectly at the corner without crossing into each other or having a gap between them.

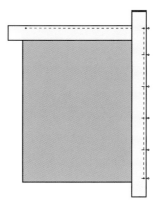

Mitering the Corner

Once you've sewn your border strips to the sides of the quilt, it's time to sew the mitered corner seams.

1. Working with one corner at a time, fold the quilt top in half diagonally, wrong sides together. Leave the border strips flat and unpressed with their right sides still against the quilt top as they were when sewn.

2. Place the border-strip tails right sides together, perfectly aligning one on top of the other. Pin the tails together so they don't shift. Pin the corner where the seams meet so that the corner is cleanly secured but not catching anything other than the tails.

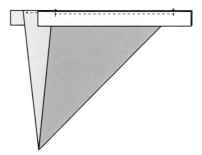

3. Place the 45° line of a ruler along the border seam. Draw a line from the interior pinned corner diagonally to the opposite corner of the border tails. This *must* be a true 45° angle for the miter to work.

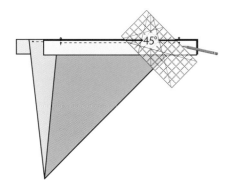

4. Sew on the drawn line. Turn the quilt top over and finger-press the border up and around the corner to check the flatness of the miter. Adjust your seam if necessary to ensure a proper flat seam. If it's too tight and bunched, take the seam out, and repeat the process, checking your accuracy each step of the way. If the seam is too floppy, use an iron to gently press in a crease to bring the corner flat. Then turn your work over and resew the seam on the crease. Once the seam is flat, cut away the excess, ¼" from the diagonal seam. Press the seam allowances open to distribute the bulk.

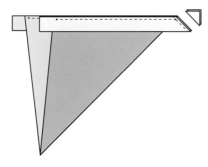

5. Repeat steps 1–4 for each of the remaining three corners.

Striped or Strip-Pieced Borders

The process for mitering simple stripes or strip-pieced borders is the same as for simple miters. The only additional step is to align the stripes or seams in step 2 of "Mitering the Corner" on page 38, and then pin them together so that they meet perfectly at the corner.

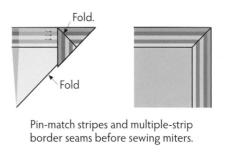

Pin-match stripes and multiple-strip border seams before sewing miters.

Mitering Corners with Border Prints

You can create some beautiful effects and visual interest by using intricate border prints in the borders of your quilt. When using this type of print, mitering allows the design to flow continuously around the corner. Generally these border prints are printed parallel to the lengthwise grain, but there are some exceptions, in which case you'll need to piece the lengths of border together before mitering. When working with border prints, I prefer to match the corners first and modify the design at the center of the strip as necessary. Some prefer to find the center for the border and let the design fall at the corners where it may. If that's your preference, follow the instructions in "Cutting Border Strips for Simple Mitered Corners" on page 37.

Examples of border prints.

The process for mitering is generally the same as a simple miter with a few additional steps and considerations. Make sure there are four full usable stripes/repeats across the width of the fabric you plan to use, and then be generous with the amount of yardage you buy. As a rule, I buy about 3½ to 4 yards of a border print so I'm sure I'll have plenty to play with.

1. Cut the border strips extra-long. A good guideline is to cut the strip the center length or width of the quilt top, plus the length of one to two full repeats of the design, plus twice the border width. Then add a few more inches for good measure. Please keep this in mind when buying border prints for a quilt. In addition, when cutting the border strips from the fabric, be sure to cut them ¼" wider than the edge of the repeat on both sides of the strip.

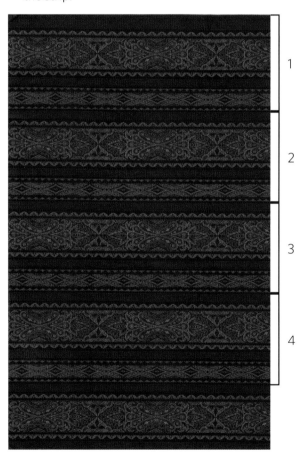

Make sure you have at least four repeats across the width of the fabric.

2. Once you've cut four super-long border lengths, it's time to preview and play with some different corner-turn options. Lay the border strip out in front of you horizontally. To preview different corner turns, flip the tail under the strip at a 45° angle at several different points in the design. This will give you an idea of what will happen at the corner at different positions on the print. Once you've found a turn you like, pin the flip in place.

Corner turn

3. Measure from the corner along the edge of the strip a distance equal to the finished center dimension of the longest quilt side. Place a pin at that mark. Moving *past* this mark further along the strip, find the same design element you chose and pin-marked for the corner turn. Flip the tail on this end up in the same way you did before, and adjust it until it's the mirror image of the first corner. Pin securely.

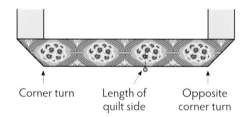

Corner turn   Length of   Opposite
              quilt side   corner turn

4. Now place the two pinned corners together to preview the full effect of how the design will turn the corner. Make any adjustments you think necessary to improve the turn.

Previewing the mitered corner.

5. Lay out the first marked strip completely over each of the other three strips and mark all corner turns, using the marked corners as a guide. It doesn't matter if your quilt sides are two different sizes, because you'll shorten them to fit both dimensions in the next steps. You can unflip the corner tails once you've pencil marked the inside point on the wrong side of the border strip at each end.

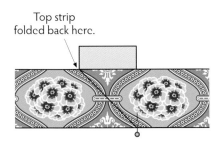

Top strip folded back here.

Use the first strip to find the correct corners on other strips.

6. Working with the side borders first, divide the finished center length of the quilt in half. For example, if the quilt top measures 60" long without seam allowances, the result would be 30". Working on the wrong side, measure in this distance (30") from each marked corner and make a pencil mark. Draw a line across the strip perpendicular to the long edge at each of these marks. Pin the back of the strip on the lines and turn it over right sides up so you can see how the repeats will play with each other at this center intersection. If it's too discordant, try shifting the seam a bit to the left or right, adding and subtracting equal amounts from the distances measured from the corners. You may find a better repeat if you measure a slightly different distance from one corner than the other, such as 28" from one corner and 32" from the other using the example given. Sometimes it takes a bit of finessing to find just the right place to put that seam. Whatever you do, the full finished center

distance of the border strip from turn to turn has to equal the finished center dimension (60") when sewn.

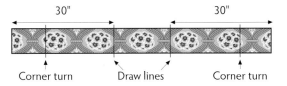

30"   30"

Corner turn   Draw lines   Corner turn

7. Place the strip right sides together, matching and pinning the drawn lines. Stitch on the line to create a center seam in your border. Trim the excess ¼" from the seam after you're sure it's where you want it. Your border strip should now measure precisely the length of the quilt side, from corner mark to corner mark.

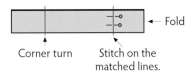

← Fold

Corner turn   Stitch on the matched lines.

8. Proceed with steps 1–4 of "Mitering the Corner" to create the mitered corner.

Mitering Odd Angles

Sometimes you'll run into a situation where you need to miter the border on a hexagonal or octagonal table topper or quilt. Because the corners aren't 90°, you need a different way to create the correct angle to sew the diagonal seam at the corners. To do so, you'll make your own custom mitering guide. With this skill, you can miter any angle correctly. You'll need graph paper, pencil, a skinny ruler, a piece of translucent template plastic, and a protractor. A protractor, used to measure angles, can be a full circle or a half circle. Don't let this intimidate you—it's not that hard at all!

Half-circle protractor

Circular protractor

Determine the Degree of the Mitering Angle

1. Begin by marking 2"- to 3"-long crosshairs ¼" in on each side of the corner to be mitered.

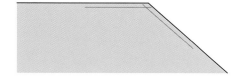

2. Now use the protractor to measure the angle. Place the crosshairs in the center of the protractor so one horizontal line is on the seam line at the corner. Orient the protractor so the 0° mark on its edge is on the left side of the same seam line.

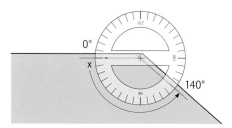

3. Measure from the 0° mark down and to the right to where the degree lines meet the ¼" seam marked on the adjacent seam. This tells you the number of degrees in the angle. In this case it's 140°.

4. Subtract the number of degrees from 360°. The result is 360° – 140° = 220°.

5. Divide the result in half: 220° ÷ 2 = 110°. This is your mitering angle.

Draw the Mitering Guide

Now you're going to make a mitering guide that equals your mitering angle (110°).

1. Draw a 6" line on a piece of graph paper. Mark the center of the line.

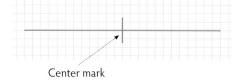

Center mark

2. Place the crosshairs of the protractor on this line so that the 0° mark is on the left side as shown.

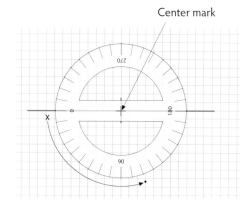

Center mark

Measure from 0° counterclockwise and mark the correct mitering angle.

3. Measure from 0° down and over to the mitering angle (110°), and make a mark on the paper.

4. Draw a line from the center point to the mark you just made. Trace the shaded area onto translucent template plastic and cut it out. Then follow the basic guidelines for a simple mitered seam on page 37. Use this guide instead of the angle line on a ruler to mark the sewing line on your border strips.

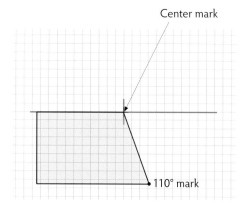

Center mark

110° mark

Pieced Borders

Pieced borders are a wonderful way to spice up your quilt. They can be very simple, from strips or squares sewn together to very complex designs. They can be straight set or composed of on-point units. No matter how simple or complex, though, accurate cutting, piecing, and pressing every step of the way is essential for the pieced border to fit onto the quilt properly. Even so, none of us is perfect and there are a few things we can do to fudge the imperfect, although only to a certain extent. Too much discrepancy cannot be made to fit.

A simple border of assorted-colored squares takes the place of a multicolored border print in "Gems."

Pieced on-point borders are a fun way to give a quilt extra pizzazz, as in this "Pine Tree" table runner.

Heavily pieced borders add to the sparkle of this quilt, called "Mountain Home."

The pieced corner squares "Mariner's Compass" add a lattice-like look to the border.

Preparing for a Pieced Border

When embarking on a quilt with a pieced border, carefully adhere to the following steps.

1. Cut all your pieces with absolute precision.

2. Sew with an accurate ¼" seam allowance.

3. Press your seam allowances carefully to avoid stretching but also to make sure all seams are flat, smooth, and crisp.

4. Check your measurements every step of the way to make sure you're on track. To do this, subtract the amount for seam allowances from the sizes you cut to determine the finished sizes of the pieces you have sewn. Once you know this, you can check all the parts for accuracy during each phase of the process. You can also add up all the finished sizes to check the accuracy of assorted pieced units as well as the completed block.

Take It Away

Different shapes I've discussed throughout the book have involved the addition of different amounts for seam allowances. Knowing how much was added to your cut pieces will aid you in knowing how much to subtract to determine the finished sizes of those pieces.

- Squares and rectangles: ½" from width and length dimensions

- Parent squares for half-square triangles: ⅞" from length of short edge

- Parent squares for quarter-square triangles: 1¼" from length of long edge

Once you've completed the center of your quilt, it's helpful to know what size it *should* be and compare those dimensions with what it *actually* measures from side to side. Once you know if there are any discrepancies between the two, you can address and fix them before you start on the borders.

To do this for straight-set quilts, calculate the quilt width by adding up the measurements of the blocks in the rows and any sashing there may be. Do the same for the length.

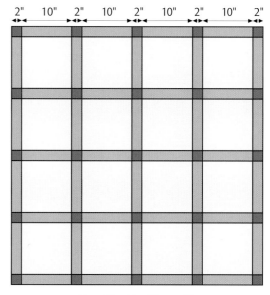

(4 x 10") + (5 x 2") = width
40" + 10" = 50"

For on-point quilt settings, you need to calculate the diagonal dimension of the various components in order to determine the finished width and length of the quilt. It's easily done with a calculator unless you're a math nut like me. Multiply the finished size of each component such as the blocks and sashing squares (if any) by 1.414. This will give you the diagonal measurement of these units. Then, using those numbers, add up the dimensions of the blocks and sashing squares across the width and length of the quilt. Let's use a quilt with 10" finished-size blocks and 2" finished-size sashing squares as an example.

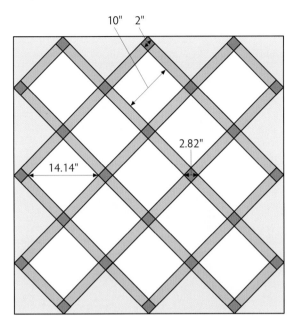

10" x 1.414 = 14.14". 2" x 1.414 = 2.828".
(3 x 14.14") + (4 x 2.828") = quilt width
42.42" + 11.312" = 53.732"

In this example, we have three quilt blocks and four sashing squares across the width of the quilt top. Multiply the block diagonal (14.14") x 3 and the sashing square diagonal (2.82") x 4 and add those two results together. The quilt width should be 57.732" or 57¾".

Once you have the finished size that your quilt top *should* measure, add ½" to each dimension and compare it with the actual measurement of your quilt through the center length and center width. If the difference is small (no more than ½"), you should be able to ease in the discrepancy. If it's larger, you may need to take in or let out some seams to get it closer to the size it should be.

Sewing Pieced Borders to the Quilt Top

The process for sewing a pieced border to a quilt top isn't that different from sewing on a plain border. Prepare the edges of your quilt top just as you would for plain borders.

1. Measure your pieced side border through the center and compare it to the center length of your quilt top. Make any adjustments necessary, referring to "Adjustment Ins and Outs" below.

Adjustment Ins and Outs

- If your border is larger than the quilt-top edge to which it will be attached, take in a tiny bit on many individual seams rather than a lot on a few. Stitch right next to the original seam so you're only taking a thread or two in on each seam. Across many seams this will add up to a decreased length, but it won't result in lopped-off points or other distortions to the piecing. Measure periodically so you don't end up taking in too much and have to rip out in reverse!

- If your border is shorter than the quilt-top edge to which it will be attached, take out a tiny bit on multiple seams. This may be tedious, but it's necessary.

2. Before sewing the adjusted pieced border to the quilt, mark its center and quarter positions. Align these with the half and quarter positions on the quilt top. An easy way to find these positions is to fold both the border and the quilt side in half, finger-press a crease, and then fold in half again and finger-press. Next, line up the creases and pin. Continue pinning the border in place, easing in small amounts of fullness as you go.

3. Repeat for the remaining borders, joining the sides first and then the top and bottom borders.

Coping Borders

Coping borders are designed to increase the size of a quilt top to a certain dimension to accommodate a pieced border of a specific size. They're often used with on-point quilt settings because these settings tend to yield quilt tops that are an odd measurement. The coping border will bring the quilt top up to something divisible by whole numbers.

Sometimes, when working with rectangular quilts, coping borders are different widths on the sides than they are on the top and bottom. This is because the quilt dimensions on all four sides must be divisible by the same number—the width of the pieced border to be attached.

The easiest way to calculate how wide to cut the coping borders is to decide what size you want your quilt top to measure to fit the pieced border. Let's look at an example using a quilt center that measures 45" x 60". Say you want to add a 4"-wide border composed of 4" pieced four-patch units. To bring the quilt center up to a measurement divisible by 4", you can add 4" finished-width strips to the top and bottom of the quilt top, increasing the 60" length to 68" (68" ÷ 4" = 17 four-patch units). For the width, you can add 3½" finished-width strips to the sides of the quilt top, increasing the measurement from 45" to 52", which is divisible by 4" as well (52" ÷ 4" = 13 four-patch units).

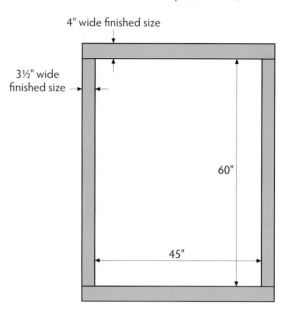

Add different-width borders to bring the quilt to a size divisible by 4".

Wow! Your quilt top is done and you're chomping at the bit to finish it up! But hold on: Before you can send it to a quilter or quilt it yourself, you need to make a backing. As one of the three layers of a quilt, the backing is just as essential to the finished project as the quilt top. Sigh. Well, backings can be fun too. So, what now?

Backings can range anywhere from plain, one-piece fabrics to another complete design option. Books have been written about reversible quilts with two design sides. Quilting two designs can be tricky, so most quilters prefer one major design side (the top) with a plain or lightly pieced paneled backing.

No matter what type of backing you plan to use, the first thing to do is determine what size it should be. To do this, measure your quilt top from top to bottom and side to side. Add anywhere from 3" to 6" to each side's measurement for a total of 6" to 12" extra in each direction. I generally add 8" (4" per side) to each dimension and plan on a backing about that size. The extra width and length allows for different rates of shrinkage caused by the fabric being drawn up during the quilting process, as well as the additional fabric that's needed to mount the quilt on a long-arm machine, if that's your quilting machine of choice.

If you plan to send your quilt to a long-arm machine quilter, consult the quilter first about preferences for extra backing and batting sizes, as well as quilt-top preparation. Follow any guidelines exactly. The professional quilter's requirements may be for more or less extra backing and batting than I've indicated, but the individual has reasons for those guidelines and will appreciate your compliance.

Plain Backings

Plain backings are composed of a single fabric, either solid or print, cut as one piece from extra-wide fabric or seamed into panels. A wide variety of extra-wide backing prints are now available, although not all quilt shops carry them. Some quilters use one-piece extra-wide cotton sateen for their backings. It's important to note that white or cream sateen or any solid fabric on the back will show every quilting stitch, whether made by hand or machine, perfect or flawed. On the other hand, a busy print will hide the quilting on the back.

One-Piece Backings

Once you know what size your backing should be, you're ready to calculate how much extra-wide backing fabric to buy. Let's say your quilt is 72" x 90". Your backing should be about 80" x 98". As an example, the extra-wide backing you're considering is 108" wide. To maximize the use of the yardage, buy enough fabric to span the narrower length of 80" and use the 108" width of fabric for the 98" dimension of the backing.

If you plan to prewash your backing, add 10% to your backing width for shrinkage (80" x 10% = 8", which when added to 80" is 88"). Divide this by 36" to calculate the yards needed (88" ÷ 36" = 2.44 yards). Round that 2.44 up to the nearest ⅛ yard, which is 2½ yards.

If you don't prewash your backing, it's still a good idea to add a few extra inches to allow for a crooked edge when the fabric is cut from the bolt. Divide whatever you decide on by 36" and round up to the nearest ⅛ yard to determine how much to buy. For instance, let's say you added 3" to the 80" dimension (80" + 3" = 83" ÷ 36" = 2.3 yards). Round 2.3 up to 2⅜ yards.

Paneled Backings

A paneled backing is pieced in two or more panels cut from 44"- or 45"-wide fabric. Depending on the size of the quilt, the panels may be horizontal or vertical to make the best use of your fabric yardage.

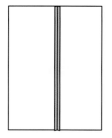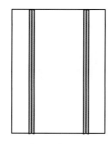

Two ways to piece vertical panels.

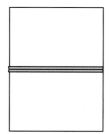

Horizontal panels

When calculating how much fabric you need, *never assume more than 40" to 42" of usable width after the selvages are removed.* Measure your intended backing so you know exactly what width it is, not including the selvages. Do *not* include selvages in any seams—remove them as you would for any piecing task.

Determine the size your backing should be by measuring the size of your quilt top and adding a total of 6" to 12"as discussed previously. Using the same quilt size as in the preceding example, 72" x 90", you'll need a backing that measures about 80" x 98". Two panels, each 40" to 42" wide, will be 80" to 84" when sewn together, which is plenty of width.

To determine the length of each panel, divide 98" by 36". The result is 2.72. Round this up to 2¾ yards. Because you'll need two panels to span the width, multiply this number by 2 (2.75 x 2 = 5.5 yards). Round this result up to the next ¼ yard and buy 5¾ yards.

If your quilt backing needs to be wider than 80", you'll need three panels, especially when you get close to a 110" width.

For smaller quilts between 40" and 70" wide, it may be more efficient to make the backing by sewing two panels with a horizontal seam, especially if the length of the quilt backing is less than 80" to 84".

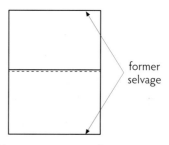

former selvage

Use a crosswise seam for backings 40" to 70" long.

In this case, suppose you want to back a lap quilt that measures 48" x 60". Your backing should be about 56" x 68". Two panels joined with a horizontal seam will be 84" long, which is more than adequate for the length. To calculate the yardage needed for each panel *width*, divide 56" by 36". The result is 1.55. Round this up to the nearest ¼-yard increment, which would be 1⅝ yards for each panel. Double this amount for two panels and buy 3¼ yards. If you were to follow the guidelines above for a vertically seamed paneled backing, you'd need 4 yards, so you save ¾ yard by making a horizontally pieced backing.

Pieced Backings

Short of making a second quilt top for the back of your quilt, there are some fun ways to use leftover prints and blocks from the front of the quilt to make a pieced back. It's a great way to use what you have on hand and cut expenses too. But, as always, you need to know the size of your backing and plan accordingly.

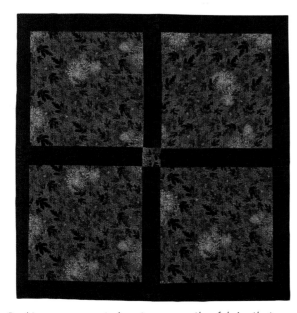

Backings are a great place to use up other fabrics that work with the quilt. This is one of my go-to backing plans that works well with many quilts. Refer to page 13 see an illustration of the front of this "Star Trails" quilt.

Here are some things to keep in mind when planning your pieced backing.

- Continue to use your best cutting, piecing, and pressing skills.

- Be sure to remove all selvages before doing any sewing.

- Avoid including any critical design element on the edges of the backing where it can be lopped off or not end up as part of the finished quilt.

- Tell your quilter if there's a center to your backing so that it can be positioned correctly. Remember to do the same if you're quilting it yourself.

- Don't heavily piece a backing or it becomes more difficult to quilt and stiff as a board when finished.

- Use extra fabrics or blocks that complement the front of the quilt and each other.

- Consider including your quilt label in the construction of your quilt back so that the quilting stitches will make the label a lasting, nonremovable part of the quilt.

Here are a few sample plans for pieced backings that I modify and use for some of my quilts. No dimensions are given because I adjust the sizes to fit the dimensions of each backing. They're just rough ideas for planning purposes only.

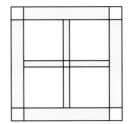

Square Backing Plan.
For longer backings, make six large square areas.

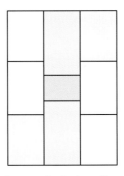

Rectangular Backing Plan.
Lengthen or widen by increasing the dimensions in the direction you want to expand.

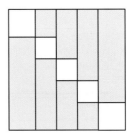

Square or Rectangular Backing Plan.
Construct in vertical bands. Add more or longer bands to increase the size.

Binding

Your quilt is quilted. To finish it, the outer raw edges of the quilt top now need to be enclosed and secured in strips of fabric called the binding. Binding strips can blend in with the outer border or become another design element of their own. They can be made from one print or many. As in any other part of the quiltmaking process, you face some important decisions.

A double-fold binding cut on the crosswise grain of fabric is the most common choice. It's a good binding to use for everything but curved edges. The double fold provides durability, while the crosswise grain has a bit of give, allowing it to handle the stretching and tugging that the edges of a quilt experience through normal use and laundering.

Sometimes it's necessary to cut binding strips on the lengthwise grain of fabric, usually because a directional print is a consideration. This type of binding won't be as durable as a crosswise-cut binding because there's no give in the lengthwise grain. It will tear easily under too much stress. Use it with caution.

Because not all quilts have square corners, it's best to use a bias binding for curved edges, because the generous give of the bias grain will allow the binding to stretch around the curves.

Linda Kittle chose to give this "Peace at Last for Carrie Nation" a scalloped edge, requiring bias binding that could bend around the curves.

For small quilts, a double-fold binding may be too thick, in which case a single-fold binding will work better. We'll cover all of these scenarios in this section.

No matter what type of binding you choose, it must be "full." This means that batting and backing must fill the inside roll of the binding completely and tightly. The reason for this actually concerns durability. A full binding wears less than a flaccid, empty binding. Therefore, some quilters won't trim the batting and backing completely even with the quilt top, instead leaving some excess to tightly fill the binding.

Note the pretty striped binding on "Tropical Stars." If the binding strips had been in the wrong direction, the stripes would be parallel to the quilt, not perpendicular as they are. Be careful when cutting directional prints for binding strips.

Calculating Binding Width

No matter what type of binding you make, you need to know how wide you want that binding to finish on the front before you can cut anything. You'll find that many patterns and books instruct you to cut binding strips anywhere from 2¼"- to 2½"-wide to make a standard ¼"-wide binding. The general rule of thumb is to cut binding strips four times the desired width for a single-fold binding or eight times the width for a double-fold binding. That would mean that for a ¼" finished binding, the strips would be cut 1" wide for single-fold binding and 2" wide for double-fold binding. Some people prefer to add up to ½" more to allow for a wide turn to the back or to allow for encasing extra-thick batting.

Some quilters prefer to cut a wider binding and sew with a ⅜"-, ½"-, or even a ⅝"-wide seam allowance so the binding is wider than ¼" on the front. Remember that seam allowance width equals finished binding width. If your outer border is unpieced, you're free to make a wider binding and use any seam allowance you wish. However, if your quilt is pieced up to the edges, you *must* use a ¼" seam allowance to attach the binding so that points or design elements aren't lopped off or distorted. You can still make a wider binding, but you'll need to use a different formula to calculate the width to cut the strips: Calculate the width of the binding as you normally would (see above) and then add four times the extra binding width beyond ¼". For instance, if you wanted a ¾"-wide finished binding on the front, subtract ¼" from ¾" for ½" and multiply the result by 4 (¾" – ¼" = ½" x 4 = 2"). Add 2" to the general binding-width formula (four times the finished binding width for single-fold binding and eight times the finished binding width for double-fold binding) and you should cut the binding strip 2" wide for single-fold binding and 4" wide for double-fold binding.

Trimming Tips

- If you're making a ¼"-wide finished binding, trim the quilt top to ¼" from any points. If you're making a wider binding, measure from any interior points and trim the backing and batting wide enough past the edge of the top to fit the extra binding width.

- If there aren't any points on the edge of the quilt, determine how much wider to cut the batting and backing by subtracting ¼" from the desired finished binding width. For example, if you want a ½"-wide finished binding, cut your batting and backing ¼" wider than your quilt top. When you sew the binding with a ½" seam allowance, your seam will fall ¼" inside the quilt top. Follow this same process no matter how wide you want your binding to be.

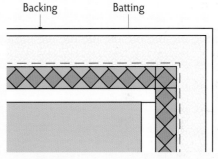

For wider binding, trim the batting and backing wider, especially if you have a pieced border.

- The other option when you have a plain, unpieced border is to trim the backing and batting even with the quilt top as usual and take in extra on the border width when you sew with the wider seam.

The binding can be a dynamic design addition, especially if you use a pieced binding or a stripe or bold print. The width of the binding in such a case must be previewed on the edge of a quilt to help you decide just how wide you want it to finish on the front of the quilt top.

Once you've decided on the finished binding width, follow these steps to prepare your quilt sandwich for binding.

1. Refer to "Trimming Tips" (page 53) for guidance on trimming the layers of the quilt sandwich.

2. Square up all corners of the quilt top.

Calculating Binding Length

Once you decide how wide to cut your binding, you need to calculate how much finished length you need.

For straight-sided quilts, including octagonal quilts or any other quilt shapes with straight edges, follow these steps.

1. Measure the length and width of your quilt top and add those numbers together. Multiply the result by 2 to yield the circumference of the top.

2. Add 12" to the result of step 1 for seams, turns, and joining the binding ends. Ta da! This is the total length of binding you need.

For scalloped edges, follow these steps.

1. Lay a piece of string around a scallop from one deep point to the next, and cut the string at the second point.

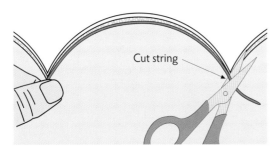

Measure the length of the curve with string.

Scrap-Happy Bindings

Sometimes it's fun to piece a binding from many prints. In that case, cut enough strips from all the prints to yield the total length you need.

The pieced binding on "Amish Puzzle" mimics the piecing used for the inner border.

2. Measure the length of the string.

3. Count the total number of scallops on the four sides of the quilt top.

4. Multiply the length of the scallop by the number of scallops and write down that number.

5. Using another piece of string, measure the curve of one corner from deep point to deep point, and cut the string at the second point.

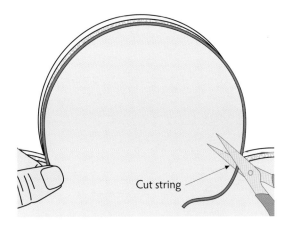

Cut string

Measure the corner in the same way.

6. Multiply the corner curve length by four.

7. Add the number from step 4 to the number from step 6, and then add 12" for seams, turns, and joining the ends. This is the total length of binding you'll need.

> ## Hexi Help
>
> If you're working with a hexagonal shape such as in a Grandmother's Flower Garden design, follow the same procedure above, measuring the length of a hexagon side, multiplying that by the number of sides on the edge of the quilt, and adding 12".

Calculating Binding Yardage

Once you know how wide and how long your binding needs to be, you can calculate how much fabric you need to buy. First, determine if you want to cut binding across the grain, on the lengthwise grain, or on the bias.

Crosswise-Cut Binding

1. Divide the length of the binding by 40" to determine how many strips you need to cut.

2. Multiply the number of strips by the strip width to get the exact number of inches you need.

3. Divide the number from step 2 by 36" to get the yardage. Round up the result to the nearest ⅛" and then add ⅛ yard. Buy this much.

Lengthwise-Cut Binding

Although this approach is rare, at least you'll know how to do the calculation if you ever need it!

1. Divide 40" by the width of the binding. This tells you how many lengthwise strips you can cut from selvage to selvage.

2. Divide the length of the binding you need by the number of strips from step 1. This tells you the length to cut each strip.

3. Round the strip length up to the nearest ⅛ yard and purchase this much fabric.

Bias Binding from a Fabric Square

If you want to make continuous bias binding, you often start with a square. Here's how to calculate the size of the square needed.

1. Using a calculator with a square-root function, multiply the length of bias binding needed by the width it will be cut.

2. Calculate the square root of this number and cut a square this size for your bias binding.

Bias Binding from Yardage

Bias binding can also be cut from regular yardage rather than a square. Here's how to calculate how much yardage is needed.

1. Using a calculator, multiply the length of bias binding needed by the width it will be cut.

2. Divide this number by 36" and cut a piece of yardage this size.

Cutting and Sewing Binding Strips

Different types of binding strips are cut and sewn in different ways.

Cutting Crosswise Strips

1. Fold and press your fabric into two or four layers as with regular rotary cutting.

2. Follow normal procedures for cutting any type of strip. Create a clean-cut edge, cut the desired strip width, and remove selvages. Refer to "Calculating Binding Yardage" on page 55 if needed to determine the number of strips.

Cutting Lengthwise Strips

1. Fold and press your fabric into 20"- to 22"-wide layers, with the selvages on the two outside edges. Work with no more than 2 yards of fabric and four layers for best results.

2. Create a clean-cut edge, removing the selvage at the same time. Cut the correct number of strips at the desired width, referring to "Calculating Binding Yardage" to determine the number of strips, if needed.

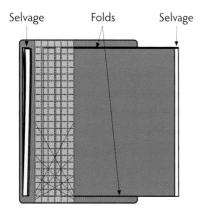

Cut lengthwise strips for directional prints.

Joining Crosswise and Lengthwise Strips

1. With the right side up, lay the tail of the first strip horizontally. Layer the second strip right side down vertically over the first strip. Leave a little excess strip length past each edge. Sew across the crossed strips diagonally. Begin and end stitching in the V formed by the excess strip lengths. Repeat until all the strips are sewn together end to end.

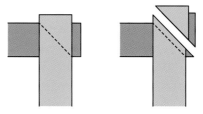

2. Trim the excess, ¼" from each seam. Press the seam allowances to one side.

3. If you're making a double-fold binding, press the long binding strip in half lengthwise, wrong sides together. For single-fold binding, leave the strip flat.

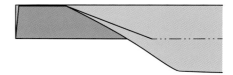

Cutting Bias Strips

1. If you're working with a square of fabric, cut from corner to corner diagonally to create two bias edges from which to cut bias strips. Proceed to step 4.

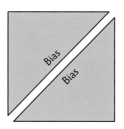

2. If you're working with a piece of selvage-to-selvage yardage for your binding, place the 45°-angle line of a long ruler on one edge of the fabric and cut along the ruler's edge. Proceed to step 4.

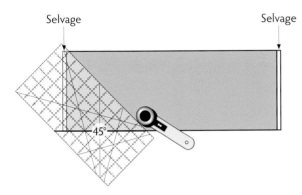

3. If you don't have a ruler with a 45°-angle line or you avoid angles because they confuse you, simply fold up one corner of the fabric onto itself so that the bottom edge meets the right edge as shown. Crease the fold, and then open the fabric back up, lay your ruler along the crease, and cut along the ruler's edge.

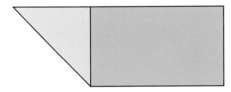

Fold and crease.

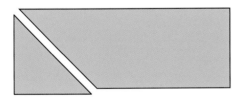

Trim on crease.

4. Measure from the cut edge to cut bias strips the width desired.

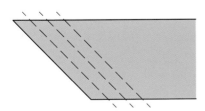

Measure from angled edge
to cut bias strips for binding.

Joining Bias Strips

1. Place two strips right sides together, offsetting the points ¼". Beginning and ending in the Vs formed by the offset, stitch the strips together.

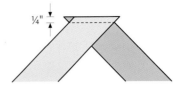

2. Lay out the strips to make sure the edges are continuous and straight. Press the seam allowances to one side.

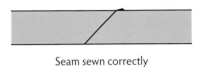

Seam sewn correctly

Seam sewn incorrectly

3. Continue adding strips in the same manner until you have one long bias strip.

4. If you're making double-fold binding, press the strip in half lengthwise, wrong sides together. For single-fold binding, leave the strip flat.

Fold and press binding strip in half
lengthwise with wrong sides together.

Making Continuous Bias Binding

1. Refer to "Bias Binding from a Fabric Square" on page 55 to calculate the size square you'll need in order to create the length of binding for your project.

2. Cut the square in half diagonally.

3. Position the triangles as shown and sew them right sides together using a ¼" seam allowance. Open out the triangles to form a parallelogram; press the seam allowances to one side.

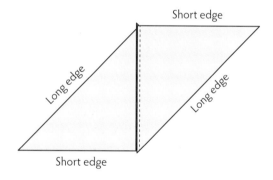

Short edge

Long edge

Long edge

Short edge

4. Using a fine-line mechanical pencil and a ruler, begin marking horizontal lines the desired cut width of the binding from the bottom up to the top along the long bias edge. Cut any excess from the top along the last line you drew. Draw a ¼" line on each short end.

Draw ¼" line from short edge.

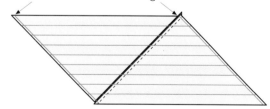

Draw lines from bottom to top
that are the width of the binding.

5. Place the two short ends of the parallelogram right sides together, matching and pinning the drawn lines where they intersect at the ¼" seams while also *offsetting the short edges by one line on the end*. Once the pieces are pinned together, they'll form a tube with lines running continuously around it.

Offset by one marked line
on each side.

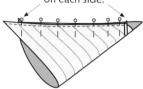

Pin two short ends of the parallelogram together.
Pin-match lines where they intersect the ¼" line to
corresponding with the intersection on other end. It
will look very "awkward." Sew on the ¼" marked lines.

6. Beginning at one offset end, start cutting on the marked lines. The cut will run continuously around the tube to the other end, creating one long bias binding strip.

Start cutting continuous
binding like an apple peel.

Sewing Binding to the Quilt Top

Sewing binding to a quilt top is fairly simple and pretty much the same for all crosswise-cut double- and single-fold binding, although there are a few differences when it comes to bias binding.

Attaching Single- or Double-Fold Binding

Follow these steps to make and attach a single- or double-fold binding to a prepared straight-edged quilt top. The binding can be cut crosswise, lengthwise, or on the bias. Let's use the example of a binding that finishes at ¼" wide and will be sewn with a ¼" seam allowance.

1. Beginning in the middle of one side of your quilt, align the raw edges of the binding with the raw edge of the quilt top. If you're working with a double-fold binding, you'll align the two raw edges. For a single-fold binding, you'll align one raw edge with the quilt top. If you're sewing a wider binding, align it with the edge of the batting and backing, which has been cut to accommodate the extra width, or align it with the edge of the quilt top if you plan to decrease the border width to allow for the extra binding.

2. Attach a walking foot to your machine, which can better accommodate the extra layers of the quilt sandwich and binding than a regular foot. Pin-mark the width of the seam allowance from the corner that you'll be sewing toward. Some walking feet now have a ¼" notch on the front that will put you exactly ¼" from the corner; if your walking foot has this feature, you don't need the pin. Leaving about 6" to 8" of the beginning tail free, sew to the pin, using a seam allowance equal to the finished width of the binding. In this

example, it would be ¼". Stop exactly at the pin-marked corner and backstitch; remove the quilt from the sewing machine.

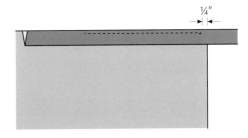

3. Flip the binding straight up from the corner so that it aligns with the next side of the quilt. Do the same even if you're working with a single-fold binding or an odd-angled corner such as a hexagonal or octagonal quilt. The key to turning any of these corners is to flip the binding straight up so it forms a continuous line with the next side.

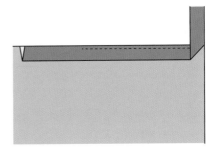

4. Now, fold the binding straight back down on itself, being careful not to move the pleat formed at the corner. By doing this, you create the correctly angled pleat in the corner to turn to the back. Pin the pleat in place. Starting at the edge, stitch the binding to the second side of the quilt top, pin-marking and stopping ¼" from the corner as before. Repeat the process for the remaining corners.

5. When you turn the last corner, sew the binding to within 12" to 18" of the starting point; backstitch and remove the quilt from the machine. If you're working with bias binding, refer to steps 6–10 of "Applying Bias Binding to Curved Edges" for instructions on joining the tails of bias-cut strips. Otherwise continue with the next step.

6. Unfold the beginning end of the binding strip and lay it flat, wrong side up. Measure from the end of the tail a distance equal to the width the binding strips were cut, and make a mark. For instance, if the binding strips were cut 2" wide, make a mark 2" in from the end of the beginning tail. Lay the marked tail out onto the edge of the quilt and pin it flat and smooth to the raw edge.

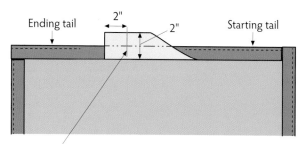

Mark distance equal to the width of the open binding.

7. Open up the end of the binding strip and lay it over the beginning of the strip, aligning the raw edges with the quilt-top edges. Pin the binding securely in place so it's as flat as it will be when sewn. Cut the ending tail at the 2" mark on the beginning tail.

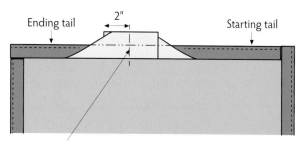

Cut the ending tail to match the mark on the starting tail.

8. Unpin the tails. Lay the tail ends right sides together at a 45° angle. Sew across the diagonal. Check to make sure the seam is correct and that the tails aren't twisted, and then trim the excess, ¼" from the seam. Finger-press the seam allowances to one side.

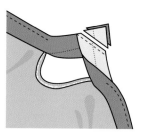

Place the starting tail and ending tail right sides together, matching corners. Sew diagonally and trim the excess ¼" from seam.

9. Place the joined binding back in position along the raw edge of the quilt top and finish sewing it in place.

Applying Bias Binding to Curved Edges

Sewing a bias binding to a curved/scalloped quilt edge isn't much different from what I've already described, but there are a few tips and tricks. A curved edge should be bound with a narrow ¼" binding. Wider bindings are more difficult to maneuver around the corners.

1. Trim the batting and backing even with the quilt top.

2. Lay the raw edges of the binding even with the quilt top on a small area. Begin on an outer edge, not at an inner point.

3. Leaving several inches of starting tail, sew slowly, pivoting frequently for deeper curves so the stitching is smoothly curved. Too many stitches lined up straight in a row will look more like a series of straight seams instead of a smooth seam. Pin if necessary to help you feel more in control.

4. Stretch the bias around the curves gently.

5. Sew slowly, stopping with the needle down at inside points. Adjust the binding around the point, lift the presser foot, pivot, and begin stitching again.

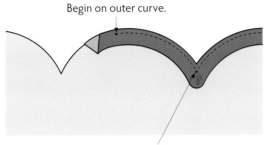

Begin on outer curve.

Stop with the needle down and pivot.

6. At the last curve, stop stitching, leaving as much work area as possible to join the tails. Open the two tails and pin them flat to the scalloped edge, with the starting tail on top of the ending tail. Tuck any excess ending tail out of the way.

7. Mark the two points of the starting tail on the ending tail.

Ending tail | Starting tail

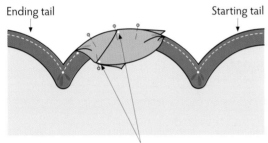

Mark the wrong side of the ending tail on both raw edges at the trimmed end of the starting tail.

8. Connect the two marks. Cut the ending tail ½" longer than the marked line. The cut should mimic the angle on the starting tail.

Ending tail | ½" | Starting tail

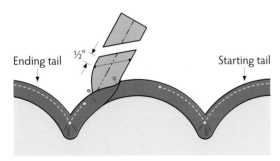

Trim the ending tail parallel to the connected marks.

9. Place the two tails right sides together. They will match wide angle to narrow point. Offset the points so that the ¼" seam will start at the V. Sew using a ¼" seam allowance.

10. Finger-press the seam allowances to one side, place the binding back in position, and stitch the rest of the binding in place.

Slipstitching Binding to the Backing

Now that the binding is sewn to the quilt top, the last step is to fold the binding over to the back of the quilt and slipstitch it in place.

1. Some people like to use clips to hold the rolled binding in place and others do without. Some people like to work with the body of the quilt on their lap and others prefer to have the quilt hang off their lap. All of these options are fine; the choice is yours.

2. Thread a hand-piecing needle with thread that matches the main color of the binding. Use no more than 18" of thread, because it will weaken as it runs back and forth through the eye of the needle. Make a small knot in one end of the thread. Slip the needle between the layers of the quilt sandwich on the back under the binding area. Come up just on the other side of the machine stitching.

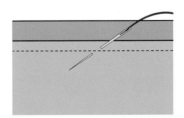

3. For a double-fold binding, roll the binding to the back so you can slipstitch through the fold. For a single-fold binding, fold the binding in half before rolling it to the back so you can slipstitch through its fold.

4. Bring the needle up through the backing at the point where the binding fold will fall next to and just below the machine stitching that attached the binding to the front. Bring the needle up from underneath, just catching the fold of the binding.

5. Now slide the needle into the backing right next to where the needle came up in the fold.

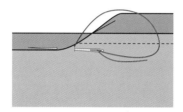

6. Take a small stitch, sliding your needle between the layers, and come back up from underneath about $\frac{3}{16}$" past the last stitch, catching just the edge of the fold at the same time. Slide the needle between the layers, not catching the fold this time, and travel another $\frac{3}{16}$" before bringing the needle back up into the fold. By stitching this way, you are coming up, catching just the fold of the binding, sliding the needle back into the layers, and traveling to the next spot before coming up to catch the fold again. Continue slipstitching the quilt along one edge until you're an inch or two from the corner. Check the front of your quilt periodically to make sure your slipstitches are not coming all the way through. If they are, take them out and redo them.

Happy Endings

End your thread well before it gets down to 6". What is left is worn from moving through the needle's eye and too weak to be useful. It's easier to end a thread when it has a little length to it. To do this, take a stitch and a backstitch. Run your needle between the layers to beneath the area that will be covered by the binding. Take another stitch and backstitch here. Form a loop with your thread and run your needle through it twice. Pull the needle through to create a small knot close to the quilt. Clip the tail. Rethread your needle and start slipstitching as before.

7. Slipstitch up to the first corner and secure the stitching with a backstitch at the machine-stitching line for the next side. Don't cut your thread, but instead park your needle in the quilt top away from the work area.

8. Fold the next side of the binding down, slipping the corner fullness under the corner to form a diagonal mitered fold. The folds should meet exactly at the corner. If you're working with a single-fold binding, be sure to fold the binding on the next side of the corner in half before rolling it to the back to form the corner miter.

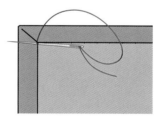

9. Slip the needle back into the layers just under the open binding fold, catching the fold on the way up. Slipstitch the open binding on the corner closed on both the front and back of the corner. End by slipping the needle to the front to start slipstitching the second side.

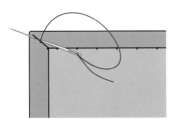

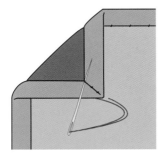

10. Continue slipstitching around your quilt top to where you started. Take your last stitch. Then take another stitch just a bit under the fold so you can hide your backstitch under the edge. Backstitch.

11. Form a loop with your thread and run your needle through it twice. Pull the needle through to create a small knot close to the quilt top.

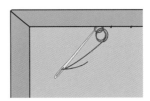

12. Slip your needle between the layers, running a distance away from the binding before pulling the needle up to the surface again. Clip your thread so the tail slips back between the layers and out of sight.

About the Author

Photography by Katie Lynn Thomas

Donna Lynn Thomas has been sewing since the age of four and quilting since 1975. She began teaching in 1981, and since 1988 she has been a National Quilting Association certified teacher for basic quiltmaking (NQACT). While an Army wife, she lived in Germany for four years and taught routinely at a quilt shop and various guilds throughout that country. Long out of the Army, the Thomases have settled in Kansas for good. Donna still teaches nationally.

Donna's many previous titles with Martingale include *Scrappy Duos*, *Flip Your Way to Fabulous Quilts*, *Patchwork Palette*, *On-Point Patchwork*, and, most recently, *Quiltmaking Essentials 1*. She has also contributed articles on various quilt-related subjects to numerous publications over the years. She is the designer of the Omnigrid On-Point Ruler.

Her greatest joy is her husband, Terry, and their two sons, Joe and Pete. Equally dear to her heart is Joe's wife, Katie, and their most-perfect-in-every-way daughters, Charlotte and Alexandra.

Donna and Terry provide staff assistance to their three cats, Max, Jack, and Skittles, and a kiddie pool and ear scratches to one sunny golden retriever, Ellie. All the quilts in their house are lovingly "pre-furred."

Visit Donna online at DonnaLynnThomas.blogspot.com.